CAUGHT With a CATCH

Poaching in Africa

Laura Layton Strom

SCHOLASTIC

This 2009 British adaptation published by
Scholastic Ltd
Villiers House
Clarendon Avenue
Leamington Spa
Warwickshire CV32 5PR

British Library Cataloguing-in-Publication Data.
A catalogue record for this book is available from the British Library.
ISBN 978-1407-10131-6

© 2009 Weldon Owen Education Limited. All rights reserved.

Author: Laura Layton Strom
Educational Consultants: Ian Morrison and Nikki Gamble
Editors: Karen Alexander, Marion Archer and Simret Brar
Designer: Emma Alsweiler
Photo Researcher: Jamshed Mistry

Photographs by: ANT Photo Library: Martin Harvey (dead rhino, pp. 20–21); NHPA (zebra herd, p. 23); Nigel Dennis (caged chimpanzee, pp. 28–29); Rik Thwaites (stuffed leopard, p. 13; lioness trophy, pp. 26–27); **Courtesy of Cheetah Conservation Fund/www.cheetah.org/© Suzie Eszterhas** (Laurie Marker, p. 5); **Dynamic Graphics** (p. 3; elephant, lion, leopard, hippo, rhino, zebra, p. 7; giraffes, p. 19); **Getty Images** (ranger with infant gorilla, p. 14); **Imagestate** (cheetah, giraffe, p. 7; hippo, p. 15; giraffe, p. 18); **Jennifer and Brian Lupton** (teenagers, pp. 30–31); **Martin Harvey/Images of Africa** (p. 22); **More Images:** FPL A (elephant and zebras, pp. 8–9; leopard and prey, p. 24); **NPL** (p. 12; dead giraffe, p. 19; charging rhino, p. 20; lion and cub, pp. 26–27); **Photodisc** (cheetah hide, fur, pp. 24–25); **Photolibrary** (elephant jawbones, pp. 14–15; pp. 16–17; rhino horns, p. 21; girl feeding elephant, rangers on watch, pp. 28–29); **Stockbyte** (rhino horns, p. 21); **Tranz/Corbis** (cover; p. 1; grazing wildebeest, pp. 8–9; pp. 10–11; golf course, p. 13; zebra skins, p. 23; leaping cheetah, p. 25; leopard claw, p. 26; butchery, pp. 30–31)

Every effort has been made to trace copyright holders for the works reproduced in this book, and the publishers apologise for any inadvertent omissions.

All illustrations and other photographs © Weldon Owen Education Limited

All rights reserved. This book is sold subject to the condition that it shall not, by way of trade or otherwise, be lent, hired out or otherwise circulated without the publisher's prior consent in any form of binding or cover other than that in which it is published and without a similar condition, including this condition, being imposed upon the subsequent purchaser. No part of this publication may be produced, stored in a retrieval system, or transmitted, in any form or by any means, electronic, mechanical, photocopying, recording or otherwise, other than for the purposes described in the lessons in this book, without the prior permission of the publisher. This book remains in copyright, although permission is granted to copy pages where indicated for classroom distribution and use only in the school which has purchased the book, or by the teacher who has purchased the book, and in accordance with the CLA licensing agreement. Photocopying permission is given only for purchasers and not borrowers of books from any lending service.

Due to the nature of the web, we cannot guarantee the content or links of any site mentioned. We strongly recommend that teachers check websites before using them in the classroom.

Teachers' notes contain extracts from Primary National Strategy's *Primary Framework for Literacy* (2006) www.standards.dfes.gov.uk/primaryframework © Crown copyright. Reproduced under the terms of the Click Use Licence.

1 2 3 4 5 6 7 8 9   9 0 1 2 3 4 5 6 7 8

Printed in China through Colorcraft Ltd., Hong Kong

CONTENTS

HIGH-POWERED WORDS	4
GET ON THE WAVELENGTH	6
On the Savannah	8
Protecting the Animals	10
Keeping the Balance	12
Poaching for Profit	14
Elephants	16
Giraffes	18
Black Rhinoceroses	20
Zebras	22
Leopards and Cheetahs	24
Lions	26
Preserving the Savannah	28
AFTERSHOCKS	30
GLOSSARY	32
INDEX	32

HIGH-POWERED WORDS

conservationist a person who works to protect plants and animals and their habitats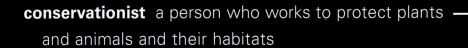

endangered close to becoming extinct

extinction the complete dying out of a species

gene the part of a cell that controls how a living thing looks and develops

habitat the area where a plant or an animal lives naturally

poacher a person who illegally kills or captures protected animals

species a group of plants or animals that share common characteristics and are able to reproduce

vulnerable exposed to the risk of being harmed

....

For easy reference, see Wordmark on back flap.
For additional vocabulary, see Glossary on page 32.

> The word *habitat* comes from a Latin word *habitare*, meaning "to live" or "to dwell". Related words include: *habitation*, *habitable* and *inhabit*.

Conservationist Laurie Marker founded the Cheetah Conservation Fund in Namibia. She was named TIME Magazine's Hero of the Planet in 2000.

Extinction can be a natural process. Over time, many **species** have become extinct. However, human activities are causing thousands of plant and animal species to become extinct.

Africa is the second largest **continent**. A large part of it is covered by grassy plains, or savannah. The savannah is rich in wildlife. But some of the savannah animals have become extinct. Many more are **endangered**.

Because of illegal hunting and other human activities, the savannah is in crisis. Many African governments, as well as a number of international organisations, are working to preserve the savannah. However, protecting the savannah and its animals has become increasingly difficult.

Every year, the International Union for the Conservation of Nature and Natural Resources (IUCN) publishes a Red List. The list tells us how close to extinction some animals and plants are. All the animals and plants on the list are in danger of extinction. Even when animals are listed as being at low risk, they are still under threat.

Red List Categories

LC	Least concern or low risk	**CR**	Critically endangered
NT	Near threatened	**EW**	Extinct in the wild (found only in zoos)
VU	Vulnerable		
EN	Endangered	**EX**	Extinct

Cheetah
- African — VU
- Northwest African — EN

Lion — VU

Elephant — VU

Rhinoceros
- Black — CR
- White — NT

Leopard — LC

Hippopotamus
- Common — VU
- Dwarf — EX
- Pygmy — EN

Giraffe — LC

Zebra
- Common — LC
- Grevy's — EN
- Mountain — EN
- Quagga — EX

On the Savannah

The sun rises on the savannah. Its rays begin to bake the dry grasses. A grey elephant and her calf lumber along. They swing their trunks to and fro. A giraffe stretches its long, delicate neck skyward. It reaches for moist, green leaves at the top of a tree. A leopard yawns as it raises its spotted head. It sniffs the air. In the distance, a lion roars. Antelope prick up their ears to listen.

A savannah is a large area of grassland. It is dotted with trees and bushes. Most savannahs are in tropical regions. However, they are also found in **temperate** regions. In Africa, a large part of the land is tropical savannah. These grasslands stretch all the way across the continent.

The African savannah is home to many kinds of animals. The grasses and trees provide food for **grazing** animals, such as antelope and zebras. The grazing animals provide food for meat-eaters, such as cheetahs and lions. Some of the savannah animals are endangered. It is illegal to kill these animals. However, that does not stop **poachers**. Their actions increase the likelihood that these rare animals will become extinct during your lifetime.

> The savannah is an ecosystem. Different species live together in a delicate balance. The balance can be easily upset by humans. Find out about the Serengeti in Kenya. Which animals live there? How do the Masai tribe live in harmony with the animals? What are the threats to their way of life?

SHOCKER
Worldwide, about 20 per cent of bird species, 25 per cent of **mammal** species, 33 per cent of **amphibians**, and 42 per cent of tortoises and turtles are in danger of extinction.

Water is precious on the African savannah. Different species of animals often join one another to drink at a water hole.

Wildebeest graze on the savannah in Kenya.

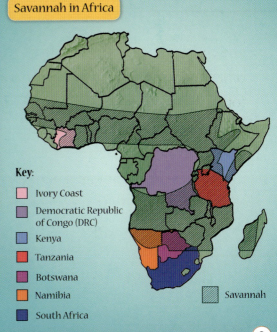

Savannah in Africa

Key:
- Ivory Coast
- Democratic Republic of Congo (DRC)
- Kenya
- Tanzania
- Botswana
- Namibia
- South Africa

Savannah

Protecting the Animals

SHOCKER
The animal species on our planet today represent only two to four per cent of all the animal species that have ever lived.

Long ago, people needed to hunt if they wanted to eat meat. Hunting is still part of some cultures. Some people hunt for food. Others hunt for sport. In the past, in Africa, tourists paid large sums of money to hunt the animals of the savannah – especially the large animals, such as lions and rhinoceroses. This brought much-needed money to the poorer countries of Africa.

Over time, hunting reduced the number of animals. At the same time, the number of humans in the region grew. Roads were built through the wild savannah. Lands were fenced to create farms. Crops were planted. Homes were built. This loss of **habitat** caused the animal populations to shrink even more.

Africa's first wildlife conservation organisation was the Natal Game Protection Association in South Africa. It was set up in 1883 to stop the savannah animals from being hunted to extinction. In 1894, the Pongola Reserve was established in South Africa as a wildlife **sanctuary**. Africa's first national park was Virunga National Park in Democratic Republic of Congo (DRC). The park was set up in 1925. There are now game reserves and national parks throughout Africa.

US president Theodore Roosevelt hunted and killed this rhinoceros in 1909.

Reserves are needed because:

- animals are hunted for food
- animals are hunted for sport
- roads are built through the savannah
- lands are fenced for farming
- homes are built on the savannah

Did You Know?

A wildlife reserve is usually set up for the protection of animals, especially endangered animals. A national park is set up to preserve the natural environment. In a national park, both the land and the wildlife are protected. People are encouraged to use the park for recreation and enjoyment.

Lions rest on road signs in the Nairobi National Park. The park's 115 square kilometres are home to 80 mammal species and 400 bird species. Set up in 1946, it was Kenya's first national park.

Keeping the Balance

Conservationists hoped that the creation of reserves would allow both animals and humans to survive on the savannah. The reserves would protect animal populations. They would also keep wild animals away from villages.

However, not everybody is happy that the reserves have been set up. Some people want to hunt animals for food. They also want to be able to earn a living by selling the meat, skin and other parts of these animals. Others want all the big **game** animals to be killed. They say that game animals eat and trample on their crops, kill their livestock and endanger their families. Some believe that the death of all big game would end the threat of disease carried by tsetse flies, which feed mainly on these animals.

Even with reserves, wild animals are not safe. Most African countries cannot afford to employ enough rangers. Poachers are able to go into the reserves and kill the animals.

SHOCKER

Tsetse flies are found only in Africa. They feed on the blood of humans and animals. The flies cause a disease in humans called sleeping sickness. It is usually fatal unless it is treated.

Poacher with elephant meat and an elephant tusk for sale

Crocodiles and golfers share the land at this golf course in South Africa.

Many leopards are killed to be sold to tourists as souvenirs.

Did You Know?

In Kenya, 42 per cent of the human population is younger than 15-years-old. In the US, only 20 per cent of the population is younger than 15. The rapidly increasing human population in parts of Africa means that the large animals of the savannah are losing their habitat.

The noun *souvenir* comes from a French verb *souvenir*, which means "to remember". So a souvenir helps us to remember something, such as a holiday.

Poaching for Profit

People poach for all kinds of reasons. Many people in Africa live in poverty. Sometimes they kill wild animals for food. One giraffe can provide a meal for everyone in a small village.

Illegal hunting is also big business. Worldwide, the illegal trade in wildlife is worth as much as £4 billion a year. Poachers collect and sell animal skins and **bushmeat**. The people who buy don't know, or don't care, that the trade is illegal. Poachers also take baby animals to be sold as pets.

One of the worst threats to the wild animals of Africa is war. One reason is that countries at war often suffer from **famine**. Famine may occur because there is no one to plant crops, or it may be caused by the destruction of crops. Another reason that war is a threat to wildlife is that armies on the move kill animals for food. Also, the sale of animal parts is a **lucrative** way for soldiers to get money for weapons.

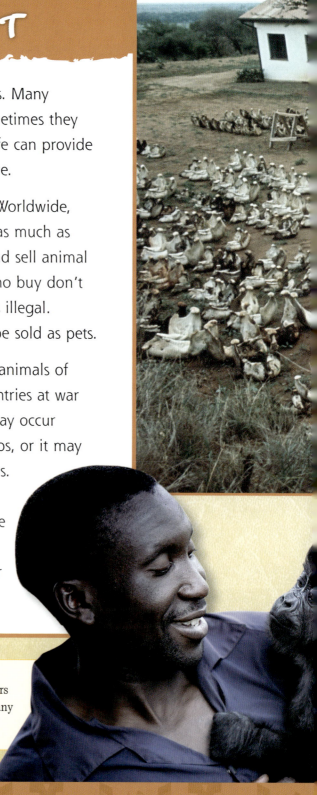

Tumaini, a baby gorilla, was rescued from poachers in the war-torn DRC. Gorillas were among the many animals killed and eaten during the war.

A collection of elephant jawbones left by poachers

SHOCKER

In 1988, there were 22,000 hippopotamuses in Virunga National Park in the DRC. At the end of 2006, after years of war, there were fewer than 400 left. Hippos were put on the IUCN Red List for the first time.

During the war in the DRC, thousands of animals, especially hippopotamuses, were killed. Park rangers were also killed. International organisations have now set up a well-armed force of 500 park rangers to protect the wildlife.

Elephants

The elephant is the world's largest land mammal. An African elephant can weigh more than 6800 kilograms. That's as heavy as five cars. It takes a lot of food to move that large body around. Elephants, which are **herbivores**, need to eat more than 140 kilograms of food a day.

Because of poaching, the African elephant is now endangered. The poachers want the long, **ivory** tusk an elephant has on each side of its trunk. Ivory has always been rare and precious. People have used it to make all kinds of objects, such as piano keys, carvings and jewellery.

In 1980, there were about 1.3 million elephants in Africa. By 1990, there were only about 609,000. In October 1989, the Convention on International Trade in Endangered Species of Flora and Fauna (CITES) banned trade in ivory. This was an attempt to protect elephants. Many countries, including Britain, do not allow elephant ivory to be imported unless it is more than 100-years-old.

The word *CITES* is an acronym – a word made up of the first letters of other words. An acronym is used to save time. For example, the acronym *NASCAR* is easier and quicker to say than <u>N</u>ational <u>A</u>ssociation for <u>S</u>tock <u>C</u>ar <u>A</u>uto <u>R</u>acing.

Many elephants have been moved to wildlife parks. However, they are still vulnerable to poachers. A single elephant tusk can sell on the illegal market for £4000.

Elephants have been hunted for their tusks for hundreds of years. The Ivory Coast in West Africa got its name because of its trade in ivory. Today, elephant tusks taken from poachers are sometimes burned in an effort to destroy the ivory trade.

SHOCKER

Despite the ban on the sale of elephant ivory, 23,000 elephants were killed in 2006 for their tusks.

Did You Know?

Vegetable ivory is a legal alternative to animal ivory. It comes from the seeds of two kinds of palm tree. The ivory-nut palm is native to South America, and the doum palm is native to the Middle East and Central Africa. The seeds are white and hard. They look very much like animal ivory.

Giraffes

Giraffes are the tallest creatures on the earth. Male giraffes can grow to be as tall as 5 metres. Because they are so tall, they need not compete with other herbivores for food. With their height, plus a 0.5-metre tongue, they can reach the leaves of tall trees. The possibility of a kick from a giraffe's powerful legs deters most **predators**. A giraffe's heart weighs about 11 kilograms. It is the size of a basketball. Special valves in a giraffe's neck help blood circulate up to its head. Giraffes can close their nostrils to keep out sand and dust.

The main threat to giraffes is humans. Giraffes are killed for their meat, skins and tails. Some people believe that a giraffe tail brings good luck. These people buy bracelets or belts made of tail hair.

Did You Know?

Giraffes have an unusual way of moving. When they walk, they move both right legs at the same time and both left legs at the same time. This is called pacing. When they run, they swing both hind legs up past their front legs. They can run at 55 kilometres an hour.

A giraffe has to spread its legs apart to reach the ground to drink. This awkward position makes it vulnerable to poachers as well as to predators. Fortunately, giraffes get most of the water they need from their food.

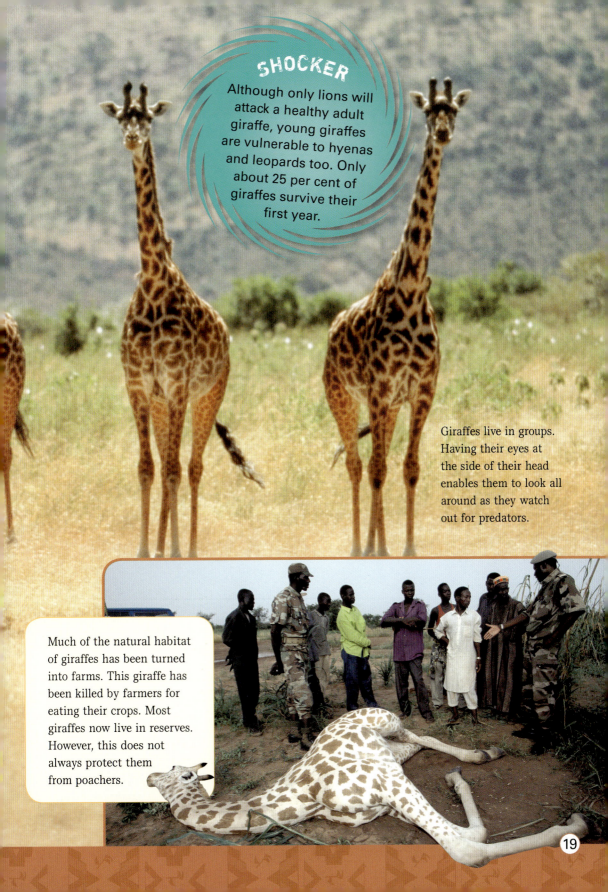

SHOCKER
Although only lions will attack a healthy adult giraffe, young giraffes are vulnerable to hyenas and leopards too. Only about 25 per cent of giraffes survive their first year.

Giraffes live in groups. Having their eyes at the side of their head enables them to look all around as they watch out for predators.

Much of the natural habitat of giraffes has been turned into farms. This giraffe has been killed by farmers for eating their crops. Most giraffes now live in reserves. However, this does not always protect them from poachers.

Black Rhinoceroses

Black rhinoceroses are actually grey. They live near water because they need to drink every day. Black rhinos browse on shrubs and trees. They can eat plants that are poisonous to other animals. They even eat burned twigs. Most black rhinos have two horns, but they can have as many as five. The front horn can grow to be one metre long.

Rhinoceroses have only one real enemy – humans. Rhinoceros horns are prized by poachers. Some horns are exported to China, where they are ground up to make traditional medicines. Some horns are used to make handles for daggers sold in the Middle East. Rhino horns have sold for £6000 on the illegal market. In 1970, there were about 65,000 black rhinos in Africa. There are now fewer than 4000.

If rhinos sense danger, they charge at high speed. Maybe this is why a group of rhinos is called a crash!

Rangers catch many poachers. But they are not always in time to stop rhinos being killed. The poachers who killed this rhino were disturbed before they could cut off its horn.

SHOCKER

A 2004 study found that seven per cent of Chinese pharmacies in New York City stocked medicines containing rhino horn. The owners said they didn't know it was illegal to use rhino horn.

Did You Know?

Rhinoceros horn is made of a fibre that is like a mixture of hair and fingernail. Some people believe that removing a rhino's horns may protect the animal from poachers. However, without a horn, a female rhinoceros can't defend her calf. Also, no one knows the long-term effects on a rhino of life without a horn.

Rhinoceros horns

Zebras

Zebras are related to horses and donkeys. They make a sound like a dog's bark. A zebra's striped coat provides camouflage. If attacked, zebras huddle together. This makes it hard for a predator to see an individual zebra. A zebra's stripes are like our fingerprints: each zebra has a unique pattern.

Great herds of zebras once roamed much of Africa. Now most zebras live in reserves. Zebras are herbivores. They need to eat for about 18 hours a day and so they require a lot of land for grazing. Therefore, they are greatly affected by loss of habitat. Poachers have seriously threatened the existence of zebras. The animals are hunted for their beautiful striped coats and for their meat.

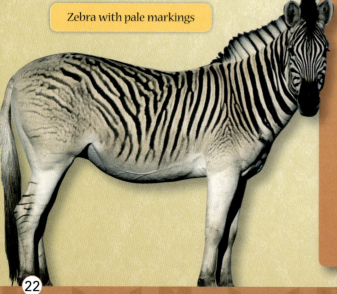

Zebra with pale markings

Did You Know?

Quaggas were a kind of plains zebra. In 1883, a quagga died at a zoo in Amsterdam. It was not until several years later that people realised she had been the very last quagga. They had been hunted to extinction! Quaggas had a striped head, neck and fore body. The rest of their body was brown with a yellow tinge. Scientists are trying to breed a zebra that looks like a quagga. They are using plains zebras that have lighter-than-usual markings on their back legs.

Zebras
- related to horses and donkeys
- herbivores
- most live in reserves
- stripes are unique
- stripes used as camouflage
- hunted for skin and meat

A zebra's stripes help protect it from non-human predators. However, its striped coat is what makes it so attractive to poachers.

Plains or common zebras

There are only three species of zebra left. Two of them, the mountain zebra and the Grevy's zebra, are very rare. There are only about 600 mountain zebras left.

Leopards and Cheetahs

Both leopards and cheetahs have beautiful spotted coats. Their coats provide great camouflage for them when they hunt. They also make them very attractive to poachers. Since 1975, it has been illegal to buy or sell leopard or cheetah skins. That hasn't stopped the poachers!

Leopards hunt at night. They are very successful predators. They will eat many types of meat. They also adapt well to different habitats, such as savannah, rainforest and desert. Because of their shrinking habitat and the actions of poachers, most African leopards now live in reserves. Although they are not considered to be facing extinction, there are very few left in the northern parts of Africa.

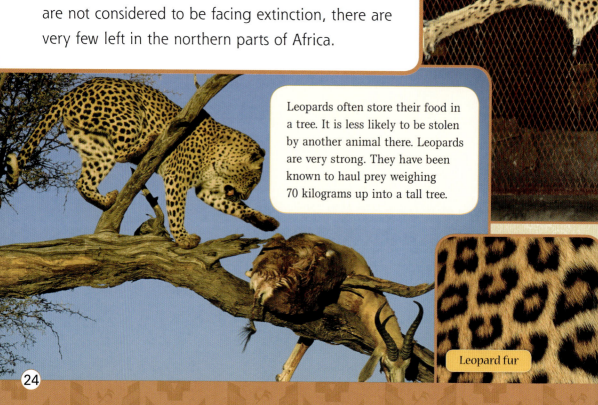

Leopards often store their food in a tree. It is less likely to be stolen by another animal there. Leopards are very strong. They have been known to haul prey weighing 70 kilograms up into a tall tree.

Leopard fur

Cheetah hide

Cheetahs are the fastest land animals. In two seconds, they can go from standing still to running at a speed of 70 kilometres an hour! They can **sprint** at 110 kilometres an hour. Unlike other cats, cheetahs cannot **retract** their claws.

Cheetahs almost became extinct 10,000 years ago. Because so few survived, they are very **inbred**. Cheetahs share 99 per cent of their **genes**. Most animal species share about 80 per cent. All cheetahs look nearly identical. Inbreeding has also reduced their **immunity** to diseases. There are fewer than 15,000 cheetahs left in the wild. Most live in Namibia, Kenya, Botswana and Tanzania. Very few cheetahs live in reserves, which means that they are very vulnerable to human activity, such as poaching and loss of habitat.

SHOCKER

It takes about seven leopard skins to make one fur coat. The United States imported more than 17,000 leopard skins between 1968 and 1969. Today, in the US, it is illegal to buy or sell a fur coat made from an endangered species.

Cheetahs' claws grip the ground just like the spikes on an athlete's shoes do. This gives them more **traction**, enabling them to run faster.

Cheetah fur

Lions

Once upon a time, lions roamed across Africa, Asia and Europe. Today, there are none in Europe and only about 200 left in Asia. Most lions in the wild live in reserves in Africa.

Lions are the only cats that live in a group. A group of lions is called a pride. On the savannah, the lionesses do most of the hunting, but the males get to eat first. The lionesses often hunt together. They encircle a herd of animals such as wildebeest. Gradually, they separate one animal from the herd. Then the lionesses close in for the kill. A male lion can eat 30 kilograms of meat in one meal, but he might not eat again for a week.

Lions are called "the king of the animals". For hundreds of years, they have been regarded as a symbol of courage. For that reason, lions have been hunted just because they are lions. They have also been hunted for their skins, or so that people can hang them on a wall as a trophy.

Claws from leopards and lions are sometimes made into jewellery. Here a lion's claw is set into a lion's head, which is carved from ivory.

There are only 200 Asian lions left in the world. They live in India's Gir Forest. Use the internet and other sources to find out about this endangered animal.

SHOCKER

About 1500 lions die each year as a result of **canned hunts** on private reserves in Africa. The semi-tame or drugged lions are put in an enclosure where they are hunted and killed. Canned hunts are legal in many places, including some US states.

Lioness trophy for sale in a store

Lion with cub

Did You Know?

The leader of a pride is usually the strongest, healthiest male. These lions generally have a splendid mane, so they are a target for trophy hunters. When poachers shoot the dominant male in a pride, they risk damaging the whole lion population. The weaker lion that takes over often kills the dead lion's cubs so that only his own cubs will survive. When this keeps happening, the species gradually becomes weaker, less healthy and less able to survive.

Preserving the Savannah

Many conservationists and animal lovers are working to save the African savannah and its animals. Organisations raise money and awareness. African governments pass laws to protect animals and habitats. Even though they are not wealthy, they help to fund and staff reserves. Poaching detectives work to catch poachers so that they can be **prosecuted**.

Rebels continue to poach animals to trade for weapons. Some people poach to avoid starvation. Africa continues to need worldwide help to preserve its savannah animals. Their loss would be a loss to the entire world.

Endangered animals are also hunted illegally in other parts of Africa and in the rest of the world. Bears are hunted for their gall bladders, which are made into traditional medicines. Sea turtles are killed for soup. Snake and lizard skins are made into shoes, handbags and belts. Birds are shot so that their feathers can decorate hats. As long as people are willing to buy objects made from wild animals, poachers will hunt the animals.

Young chimpanzee waiting to be sold as a pet or as food

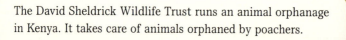

The David Sheldrick Wildlife Trust runs an animal orphanage in Kenya. It takes care of animals orphaned by poachers.

SHOCKER

In just one week in 2005, the International Fund for Animal Welfare found more than 9000 live wild animals or wild-animal products for sale on the internet.

Did You Know?

An international organisation called TRAFFIC keeps track of trade in wildlife products. TRAFFIC stands for Trade Records Analysis of Flora and Fauna in Commerce. In the United States, imports are regulated by the US Fish and Wildlife Service and US Customs.

Savannah Poaching

- elephant – ivory tusks
- giraffe – meat, skin, tail
- black rhino – horns
- zebra – skin, meat
- leopard/cheetah – skin
- lion – skin, trophies

Rangers use global positioning system receivers to track endangered animals. The vast size of the parks makes it impossible to stop all poaching.

Kenya, in Africa, does not allow the hunting of wild animals for sport. However, some landowners would like to change the law. They want to let tourists pay to hunt non-protected wild animals on their property. They say that the animals kill their livestock and threaten the safety of their families. The landowners are not suggesting that endangered animals be killed.

WHAT DO YOU THINK?

Do you think Kenya's farmers should have the right to let tourists kill wild animals on the farmers' own property?

PRO

People have a right to protect their property and their family. They also have the right to earn money for their family. Other places allow the hunting of animals that aren't under threat. Also, the money would help to save animals that are endangered.

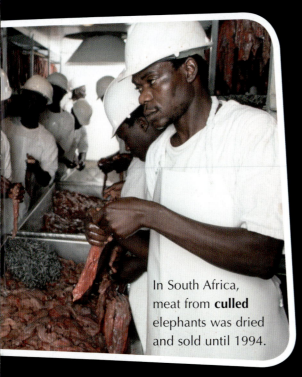

In South Africa, meat from **culled** elephants was dried and sold until 1994.

The landowners argue that Kenya is a poor country. People need the money that hunting safaris would bring. The landowners also say that the cost of conservation is greater than the amount of money currently earned from tourism. By selling hunting rights, they would be able to contribute more money to animal sanctuaries.

CON

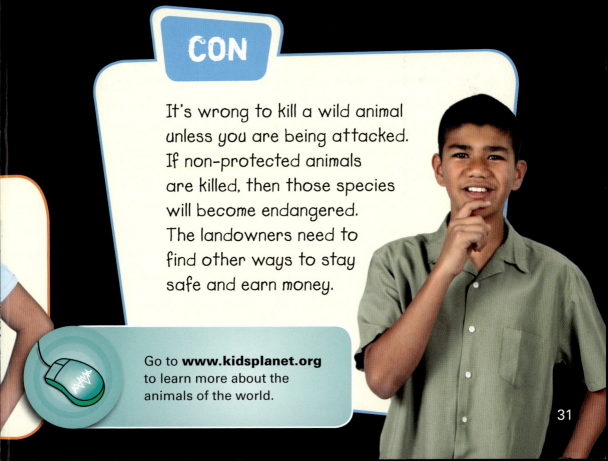

It's wrong to kill a wild animal unless you are being attacked. If non-protected animals are killed, then those species will become endangered. The landowners need to find other ways to stay safe and earn money.

Go to **www.kidsplanet.org** to learn more about the animals of the world.

GLOSSARY

amphibian an animal, such as a frog, that lives part of its life in water and part on land

browse to eat twigs, leaves and shrubs

bushmeat the meat of wild animals

camouflage the colour or shape of an animal that helps it blend in with its surroundings

canned hunt the hunting of wild animals within a restricted area from which they cannot escape

continent one of the seven main land masses that make up the earth

cull to kill weakened animals in order to maintain a healthy population

famine an extreme shortage of food

game a wild animal that is hunted for sport or food

graze to eat grass

herbivore a plant-eating animal

immunity the body's ability to fight off disease

inbred having produced offspring by mating with a close relative

ivory the material of which the tusks of elephants and some other animals are made

lucrative well-paying

mammal a warm-blooded animal that nurses its young

predator an animal that hunts and eats other animals

prosecute to take legal action against a person for a crime

rebel a person who fights against the government

retract to draw back in

sanctuary a place where animals are protected

sprint to run fast for a short distance

temperate having warm summers and cold winters

traction the gripping power that keeps something from slipping

unique unlike anything else; one of a kind

INDEX

camouflage	22–24
conservation	5–6, 10, 12, 28, 31
endangered	6–8, 11, 25, 28–31
extinction	6–8, 10, 22, 24–25, 27–28
governments	6, 28
habitats	6, 10, 13, 19, 22, 24–25, 28
herbivores	16, 18, 22
hunting	6, 10–12, 14, 17, 22–24, 26–28, 30–31
illegal trade	14, 16, 20, 24–25, 28
ivory	16–17, 26
medicines	20–21, 28
predators	18–19, 22–24
Red List	6–7, 15
reserves	10–12, 19, 22, 24, 26–28
tourists	10, 13, 30–31